KOTOWAZA

Japanese Proverbs and Sayings

Clay & Yumi Boutwell

Published by Kotoba Books
www.Kotobainc.com

Visit **http://www.TheJapanShop.com** for quality Japanese language learning materials.

ISBN: 1481904310
ISBN-13: 978-1481904315

CONTENTS

諺

KOTOWAZA

Proverbs are often thought of as clichés—albeit clichés with a poetic touch. Proverbs, however, are far from meaningless and overused phrases. They often express in a compact and precise way complex thoughts that would otherwise require a great deal of explanation.

Japanese tend to use *kotowaza* often—more often than most English speakers. It would therefore be beneficial for you to pepper your vocabulary with these pithy pieces of wisdom. The fifty proverbs contained in this book represent some of the most useful *kotowaza* heard in Japanese daily life.

You'll notice them in movies, in writing, and most importantly spoken by friends and colleagues. Knowing common *kotowaza* will not only help you express your thoughts more clearly, but also take your Japanese to a whole new polished level.

As they say, 「善は急げ」 [see page 24]

So let's get started...

諺 猫に小判
Cast Pearls Before Swine

Japanese	ねこ に こばん *neko ni koban*
Literal	Give money to a cat.
Similar to	To cast pearls before swine.

- 猫に *neko ni* (give) to a cat [に shows direction]
- A 小判 *koban* was an oval-shaped gold coin used during the Edo period.
- 豚に真珠 *buta ni shinju* Pearls to a pig. This proverb from the Bible is also often heard in Japanese and means basically the same thing as 猫に小判.

諺 猫に小判

Cast Pearls Before Swine

宝石(ほうせき)に興味(きょうみ)のない人(ひと)に

ダイヤモンドを

上(あ)げても、**猫(ねこ)に小判(こばん)だ。**

houseki ni kyoumi no nai hito ni daiyamondo wo agetemo, neko ni koban da.

For someone who has no interest in precious stones, even giving that person a diamond would be casting pearls before swine.

宝石 *houseki*—precious stones; gems

興味のない人 *kyoumi no nai hito*—a person not interested in…

に *ni*—indicates the 興味のない人 is the receiver of ダイヤモンド

ダイヤモンド *daiyamondo*—diamond

上げても *agete mo*—even if you give (him a diamond)

諺 口は禍のもと

The Mouth is a Gate of Misfortune

Japanese	くち　は　わざわい　の　もと *kuchi wa wazawai no moto*
Literal	The mouth is the beginning of disasters.
Similar to	The mouth is a gate of misfortune.

- This is sometimes written with the kanji 災い *wazawai*. Either way is fine and both mean the same thing.
- もと *moto* means origin or source; a common expression in Japanese is もともと to mean "previous": もともとの仕事 *moto moto no shigo-to* — previous work

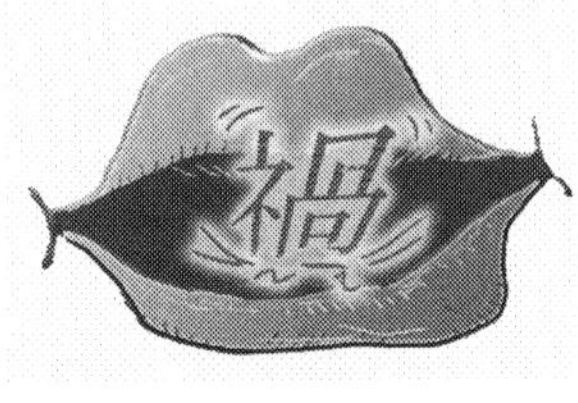

諺 口は禍のもと
The Mouth is a Gate of Misfortune

口(くち)**は 禍**(わざわい)**のもと**だから、噂話(うわさばなし)は

やめたほうがいい。

kuchi wa wazawai no moto dakara, uwasa banashi wa yameta hou ga ii.

The mouth is the beginning of disasters, so you should stop gossiping.

口 *kuchi*—mouth

禍 *wazawai*—calamity; evil; trouble

もと *moto*—origin; beginning

だから *dakara*—so; therefore; accordingly

噂話 *uwasa banashi*—gossiping; rumor

やめたほうがいい *yameta hou ga ii*—It would be better to stop [~ほうがいい is a useful construction meaning "It would be better to..."]

諺 塵も積もれば山となる

Many a Little Makes a Mickle

Japanese	ちり　も　つもれば、やま　と　なる *chiri mo tsumoreba, yama to naru*
Literal	Even dust when piled up becomes a mountain.
Similar to	Many a little makes a mickle.

- "Mickle" means "a large amount."
- 積もる *tsumoru*—accumulate; pile up [積もった雪 *tsumotta yuki* piled-up snow]
- ～れば ~*reba*—makes a conditional "if" or "even when…"
- ～となる ~*to naru*—becomes

諺 塵も積もれば山となる

Many a Little Makes a Mickle

ちり　つ　やま

塵も積もれば山となるというから、

まいにち　えん　ちょきん

毎日１０円ずつ貯金しよう。

chiri mo tsumoreba yama to naru to iu kara, mainichi juu en zutsu chokin shiyou.

Even dust, when piled up, becomes a mountain. So, let's save 10 yen a day.

塵 *chiri*—dust

積もれば *tsumoreba*—if you pile up; if you accumulate

山 *yama*—mountain

となる *to naru*—becomes

という *to iu*—they say [という is used after quotes: called…; known as...]

から *kara*—therefore; because of that

毎日 *mainichi*—everyday

１０円ずつ *juu en zutsu*—10 yen a piece

貯金 *chokin*—savings

諺 出る杭は打たれる

Don't Stick Out

Japanese	でる　くい　は　うたれる *deru kui wa utareru*
Literal	The nail that sticks out will be hammered.
Similar to	Don't stick out.

- 出る *deru*—to leave; appear [by implication, to stick out]
- 杭 *kui*—a nail
- 打たれる *utareru*—to be beaten; be hit; be struck [むちで打たれる *muchi de utareru*—to be lashed with a whip; 音楽に打たれる *ongaku ni utareru*—to be hit (moved) by music]

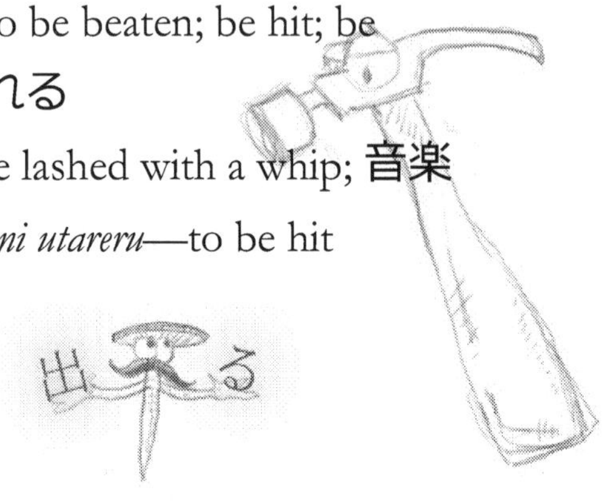

諺 出る杭は打たれる

Don't Stick Out

出る杭は打たれるから、あまり目立ったことはしないほうがいい。

deru kui wa utareru kara, amari medatta koto wa shinai hou ga ii.

The nail that sticks up gets hammered. It would be better to not do anything to draw attention.

出る *deru*—sticking up
杭 *kui*—nail
打たれる *utareru*—gets hammered
から *kara*—because
あまり *amari*—not too much [followed by a negative verb: あまり・・・しない]
目立ったこと *medatta koto*—something that stands out; conspicuous
しないほうがいい *shinai hou ga ii*—be better to not do...

諺 親しき仲にも礼儀あり

Always Care about your Flowers & Friends

Japanese	したしき　なか　にも　れいぎ　あり *shitashiki naka nimo reigi ari*
Literal	Even among close friends, there is etiquette.
Similar to	Always care about your flowers and your friends. Otherwise, they'll fade and soon your house will be empty.

- 親しい *shitashii*—familiar; close; intimate
- 仲 *naka*—relations; relationship
- にも *ni mo*—even
- 礼儀 *reigi*—courtesy; etiquette; civility

おはようございます
おばあさま

諺 親しき仲にも礼儀あり

Always Care about your Flowers & Friends

家族(かぞく)でもちゃんとあいさつをしなさい。**親(した)しき仲(なか)も礼儀(れいぎ)ありだ。**

kazoku demo chanto aisatsu wo shinasai. shitashiki naka nimo reigi ari da.

Even if it is just family, say your greetings properly. Even among relations, there is etiquette.

家族 *kazoku*—family

でも *de mo*—even

ちゃんと *chanto*—exactly; correctly; properly

あいさつ *aisatsu*—greeting; salutation

しなさい *shinasai*—do (the greetings)

諺 朱に交われば赤くなる

He that Touches Pitch Shall be Defiled

Japanese	しゅ　に　まじわれば　あかく　なる *shu ni majiwareba akakunaru*
Literal	Anything you mix with red, becomes red.
Similar to	He that touches pitch shall be defiled.

- 朱 *shu*—cinnabar red (the color of a bright red mineral)
- 交われば *majiwareba*—if mixed up with
- 赤くなる *akaku naru*—become red

諺 朱に交われば赤くなる

He that Touches Pitch Shall be Defiled

ともだち　さそ　かれ
友達に誘われて、彼はまた

わる
悪いことをしたらしい。

しゅ　まじ　あか
朱に交われば赤くなるだ。

tomodachi ni sasowarete, kare wa mata warui koto wo shita rashii.
shu ni majiwareba akaku naru da.

Being invited by a friend (bad influence), it looks like he's done another bad thing. He who keeps company with wolves will learn to howl!

友達 *tomodachi*—a friend
誘われて *sasowarete*—was invited (passive)
彼 *kare*—he
また *mata*—again
悪いこと *waruikoto*—a bad thing
らしい *rashii*—it seems; looks like

諺 急がば、回れ
Make Haste Slowly

Japanese	いそがば、　まわれ *isogaba, maware*
Literal	If you are in a hurry, take the long route.
Similar to	Make haste slowly; better to go about than to fall into the ditch.

- When in a hurry with important or dangerous tasks, taking the long but safe path may actually be speedier than the shortcuts.
- 急がば *isogaba*—if you hurry
- 回れ *maware*—run in circles; rotate; spin [But here it means to take the long way around and not necessarily to run in a circle]

諺 急がば、回れ

Make Haste Slowly

車(くるま)で行(い)くより、少(すこ)し遠(とお)いけど、駅(えき)から電車(でんしゃ)で行(い)ったほうがいい。

急(いそ)がば回(まわ)れだ。

kuruma de iku yori, sukoshi tooi kedo, eki kara densha de itta hou ga ii. isogaba maware da.

Instead of going by car, even though it is a little longer, you should go by train from the station. Make haste slowly.

車で *kuruma de*—by car

行く *iku*—to go

より *yori*—less than [used to show comparison between two things; the phrase before より is what is less desired]

少し遠い *sukoshi tooi*—a little far

けど *kedo*—but

駅から *eki kara*—from the station

電車で *densha de*—by train

行ったほうがいい *itta hou ga ii*—It would be better to go...

諺 石の上にも三年

Perseverance Brings Success

Japanese	いし　の　うえ　にも　さんねん *ishi no ue nimo sannen*
Literal	Three years on top of even a (cold) stone (will warm it).
Similar to	Perseverance brings success.

- Even the coldest rock will warm if sat on for three years.
- 石 *ishi*—rock; stone
- の上にも *no ue ni mo*—even on top of…
- 三年 *san nen*—three years

諺 石の上にも三年

Perseverance Brings Success

今(いま)は仕事(しごと)が大変(たいへん)だろうけど、**石(いし)の上(うえ)にも三年(さんねん)**だ。最低(さいてい)3年間(ねんかん)はがんばって。

ima wa shigoto ga taihen darou kedo, ishi no ue nimo sannen da. saitei sannenkan wa ganbatte.

I'm sure work is really busy right now, but perseverance brings success. Keep at it at least three more years.

今 *ima*—now
仕事 *shigoto*—work
大変 *taihen*—serious; terrible; awful; busy
だろう *darou*—I think; I suppose
けど *kedo*—but
最低 *saitei*—minimum; lowest
3年間 *san nenkan*—three years' time
がんばって *ganbatte*—keep at it

諺 善は急げ

Strike while the Iron is Hot

Japanese	ぜん　は　いそげ *zen wa isoge*
Literal	Hurry to do good.
Similar to	Strike while the iron is hot.

- 善 *zen*—good; goodness; virtue
- 急げ *isoge*—hurry up; quick to do

諺 善は急げ

Strike while the Iron is Hot

これはいいチャンスだ。

善(ぜん)は急(いそ)げ。すぐに出発(しゅっぱつ)しよう。

kore wa ii chansu da. zen wa isoge. sugu ni shuppatsu shiyou.

This is a great chance! Strike while the iron is hot. Let's go.

これ *kore*—this

いいチャンス *ii chansu*—a good chance

すぐに *sugu ni*—at once; immediately

出発しよう *shuppatsu shiyou*—let's leave

諺 犬猿の仲

Cat and Dog Terms

Japanese	けん　えん　の　なか *ken en no naka*
Literal	Relations between dogs and monkeys.
Similar to	To be on cat-and-dog terms.

- 犬 *ken* dog [the kun reading and most used is いぬ *inu*]
- 猿 *en* monkey [the kun reading and most used is さる *saru*]
- 仲 *naka* relations; relationship [Don't confuse this with 中 *naka*, meaning "middle."]

諺 犬猿の仲

Cat and Dog Terms

Aさんと Bさんは、いつも仲(なか)が悪(わる)い。**犬猿(けんえん)の仲(なか)だ。**

A san to B san wa, itsumo naka ga warui. ken en no naka da.

A and B are always at each other's throat just like cats and dogs.

Aさん *A san*—Mr. A

と *to*—and

Bさん *B san*—Mr. B

いつも *itsumo*—always

仲が悪い *naka ga warui*—not on good terms

諺 鬼の目にも涙

Even the Hardest Heart will at times Feel Pity

Japanese	おに　の　め　にも　なみだ *oni no me nimo namida*
Literal	Even in the eyes of ogres, there are tears.
Similar to	Even the hardest heart will sometimes feel pity.

- 鬼 *oni*—ogre; demon; a fiend
- 目 *me*—eye
- にも *nimo*—even
- 涙 *namida*—tears

諺 鬼の目にも涙

Even the Hardest Heart will at times Feel Pity

な
あのこわもてのＣさんが泣く

おに　め　なみだ
なんて、**鬼の目にも 涙**だ。

ano kowamote no C san ga naku nante, oni no me ni mo namida da.

For that fearful bully Mr. C to cry, why it just goes to show even the hardest heart will sometimes feel pity.

あの *ano*—that

こわもて *kowamote*—feared and respected

の *no*—possessive particle

Ｃさん *C san*—Mr. C

泣く *naku*—to cry

なんて *nante*—shows emphasis [ex. 彼**なんて**大嫌い！ *kare* **nante** *daikirai* I **really** hate him.]

諺 花より団子

Bread is Better than the Song of Birds

Japanese	はな　より　だんご *hana yori dango*
Literal	Food is better than flowers.
Similar to	Bread is better than the song of birds.

- To be practical and less concerned with appearances
- 花 *hana*—flowers
- より *yori*—less than (flowers are less important…)
- 団子 *dango*—Japanese dumpling; boiled or steamed ball of rice flour (food)

諺 花より団子

Bread is Better than the Song of Birds

買(か)い物(もの)に行(い)くより、レストランに行(い)きたいなんて、**花(はな)より団子(だんご)**だね。

kaimono ni iku yori, resutoran ni ikitai nante, hana yori dango da ne.

Wanting to go to the restaurant more than shopping—Why, you are just too practical.

買い物 *kaimono*—shopping

に行く *ni iku*—to go~ (shopping)

より *yori*—less than [used to show comparison between two things; the phrase before より is what is less desired]

レストラン *resutoran*—restaurant

に行きたい *ni ikitai*—want to go to… [the word before に shows where]

なんて *nante*—shows emphasis [ex. 彼が犯人だ**なんて**信じられません。 *kare ga hannin da* ***nante****, shinjiraremasen.* I **just** can't believe he is the criminal.]

諺 目からうろこが落ちる

Scales Falling from my Eyes

Japanese	め　から　うろこ　が　おちる *me kara uroko ga ochiru*
Literal	Scales fall from the eyes.
Similar to	Scales fall from the eyes.

- To have a sudden revelation of the truth—from the book of Acts in the Bible
- 目から *me kara*—from the eye
- うろこ *uroko*—scales (of a fish)
- 落ちる *ochiru*—to fall

諺 目からうろこが落ちる

Scales Falling from my Eyes

先生（せんせい）の 話（はなし） を聞（き）いて、

目（め）からうろこが落（お）ちた。

sensei no hanashi wo kiite, me kara uroko ga ochita.

Listening to my teacher, it was like scales falling from my eyes.

先生 *sensei*—teacher

話 *hanashi*—talk; speech

聞いて *kiite*—listening

諺 起承転結

Don’t put the Cart before the Horse

Japanese	き しょう てん けつ *ki shou ten ketsu*
Literal	Introduction, development, turn, and conclusion
Similar to	Don’t put the cart before the horse.

- The order is important.
- A story has a beginning (起) , develops (承) , then turns (転) , and is followed by a conclusion (結) .

諺 起承転結

Don't put the Cart before the Horse

しょうせつ　か
小説を書くときは、
きしょうてんけつ　たいせつ
起承転結が大切だ。

shousetsu wo kaku toki wa, kishou tenketsu ga taisetsu da.

When writing a novel,
the order of things is important.

小説 *shousetsu*—a novel

書くとき *kakutoki*—when writing

大切 *taisetsu*—important

諺 神出鬼没

To Appear and Disappear like a Phantom

Japanese	しん しゅつ き ぼつ *shin shutsu ki botsu*
Literal	Appearing in unexpected places at unexpected moments.
Similar to	To appear and disappear like phantoms.

- For someone to suddenly appear like a phantom and then disappear.
- To have complete control of movements and be difficult to catch.

諺 神出鬼没

To Appear and Disappear like a Phantom

かいとう　　　　　　　　　　あらわ
怪盗ルパンは、いつどこに現れ

しんしゅつきぼつ
るかわからない。**神出鬼没**だ。

kaitou rupan wa, itsu doko ni arawareru ka wakaranai. shinshutsu ki-botsu da.

There's no telling when or where the mysterious thief Rupan will appear. He's like a phantom.

怪盗 *kaitou*—mysterious thief

ルパン *rupan*—a name; Lupan

いつどこに *itsu doko ni*—whenever, at any place

現れる *arawareru*—appear; come out

か *ka*—shows uncertainty

わからない *wakaranai*—don't know

諺 十人十色

Different Strokes

Japanese	じゅう にん と いろ *juu nin to iro*
Literal	Ten people, ten colors
Similar to	Different strokes for different folks.

- Note the 人 kanji (person) uses two different readings: first, じゅう and then と; The most common reading is ひと, though.
- 色 *iro* color—here means "preferences" or "likes".

諺 十人十色

Different Strokes

ひと　この　じゅうにんといろ
人の好みは、**十人十色**だ。

hito no konomi wa, juunintoiro da.

Everyone has their own likes.

人 *hito*—person; people

好み *konomi*—likes; tastes

諺 前人未到

Untrodden and Unexplored

Japanese	ぜん　じん　み　とう *zenjin mitou*
Literal	An area untrodden by previous people
Similar to	Untrodden and unexplored

- 前人 *zenjin*—predecessors; people of the past
- 未 *mi*—not yet
- 到 *tou*—lead; reach; go

諺 前人未到

Untrodden and Unexplored

あの人(ひと)は、**前人未到**(ぜんじんみとう)の偉業(いぎょう)を成(な)し遂(と)げた。

ano hito wa, zenjin mitou no igyou wo nashi togeta.

That person has accomplished great exploits never attempted by others.

あの人 *ano hito*—that person

偉業 *igyou*—a great achievement; a great feat

成し遂げた *nashi togeta*—accomplish; achieve; complete

諺 自由自在

Free as a Bird

Japanese	じ ゆう じ ざい *jiyuu jisai*
Literal	Freedom and free
Similar to	Free as a bird

- 自由 *jiyuu*—freedom; liberty [自由時間 *jiyuu jikan*—free time; time to do what you wish]
- 自在 *jizai*—able to do as one desires [日本語を自在に話せる *nihongo wo jizai ni hanaseru*—To be able to speak Japanese freely]

諺 自由自在

Free as a Bird

あのシェフは、

じゆうじざい　ほうちょう　つか
自由自在に包丁を使う。

ano shefu wa, jiyuujizai ni houchou wo tsukau.

That chef uses his knife with perfect freedom.

あの *ano*—that

シェフ *shefu*—chef

自由自在に *jiyuujizai ni*—freely

包丁 *houchou*—knife

使う *tsukau*—use

諺 悪戦苦闘

Hard Fighting

Japanese	あく　せん　く　とう *akusen kutou*
Literal	Hard fighting, hard struggle
Similar to	Fight Tooth and Nail; Fight with one's Back to the Wall

- 悪 *aku*—bad; evil
- 戦 *sen*—war
- 苦闘 *kutou*—struggle; a hard fight [海流に苦闘する *kairyuu ni kutou suru*—to struggle against the (ocean) current]

諺 悪戦苦闘

Hard Fighting

強敵(きょうてき)を相手(あいて)に**悪戦苦闘**(あくせんくとう)する。

kyouteki wo aite ni akusenkutou suru.

The formidable enemy made his opponent struggle hard.

強敵 *kyouteki*—strong enemy

相手 *aite*—partner; companion

諺 大胆不敵

The Brave and the Bold

Japanese	だい たん ふ てき *daitan futeki*
Literal	Audacious and daring; to be fearless
Similar to	The bold and the brave

- 大胆 *daitan*—bold; daring
- 不敵 *futeki*—means fearless; daring, but to help remember it, it is 不 *fu*—not; un- + 敵 *teki*—enemy. There is no enemy who can conquer the fearless.

諺 大胆不敵

The Brave and the Bold

だいたんふてき　こうどう
大胆不敵な行動をとる。

daitanfuteki na koudou wo toru.

To have audacious behavior.

行動 *koudou*—behavior; action

とる *toru*—take [used with 行動 often to mean "to have such behavior" or "to take to such a behavior"]

諺 以心伝心

Heart to Heart

Japanese	い しん でん しん *ishin denshin*
Literal	By means of the mind; connect with mind
Similar to	Heart to heart; telepathy

- 以 through; by means of
- 心 heart; mind
- 伝 communication; relay

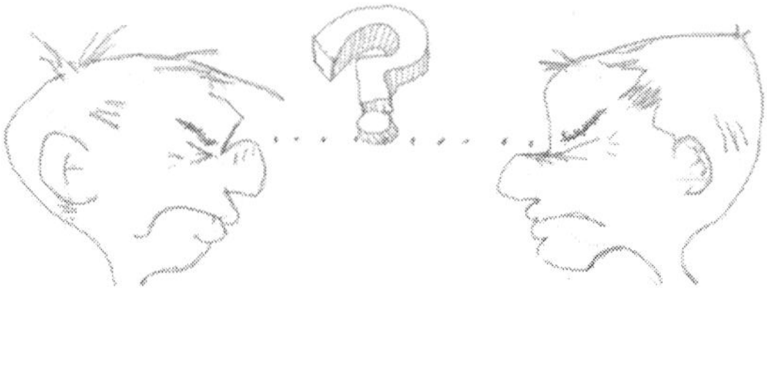

諺 以心伝心

Heart to Heart

おっと　い
夫の言いたいことは、

いしんでんしん
以心伝心でわかる。

otto no iitai koto wa, ishindenshin de wakaru

I know what my husband wants to say before he says it.

夫 *otto*—husband

言いたいこと *iitai koto*—what (he) wants to say

でわかる *de wakaru*—by (*ishindenshin*) I understand

諺 一網打尽

Catch all at Once

Japanese	いち もう だ じん *ichimou dajin*
Literal	With one net, catch all
Similar to	Wholesale arrest; get all with one strike

- Often this is used in the context of police catching criminals—a wholesale arrest; arrest in one swoop

諺 一網打尽

Catch all at Once

けいさつ　　どろぼう　　いちもうだじん
警察は、泥棒たちを**一網打尽**にした。

keisatsu wa, dorobou tachi wo ichimou dajin ni shita.

The police netted the whole gang of robbers in one fell swoop.

警察 *keisatsu*—police

泥棒たち *dorobou tachi*—robbers (たち makes it plural)

にした *ni shita*—the "ni" shows by which way it was done: by *this* way were the robbers caught.

諺 矛盾

Out of the Mouth Blows Hot and Cold

Japanese	む　じゅん *mujun*
Literal	Spear and shield [but means a contradiction]
Similar to	Out of the mouth blows hot and cold.

As the story goes, there was a weapons dealer who sold spears (矛 *hoko*) that could pierce through any shield. He also sold shields (盾 *tate*) that could withstand any spear. Someone asked if his spear could pierce his shield. The dealer couldn't answer, hence a contradiction or inconsistency.

諺 矛盾

Out of the Mouth Blows Hot and Cold

かれ　せつめい　むじゅん
彼の説明には、**矛盾**がある。

kare no setsumei ni wa, mujun ga aru.

His explanation has an inconsistency.

彼の *kare no*—his [*kare* he + *no* possessive = his]

説明 *setsumei*—explanation

矛盾がある *mujun ga aru*—there is a contradiction

諺 光陰矢の如し

Time Flies Like an Arrow

Japanese	こういん　や　の　ごとし *kouin ya no gotoshi*
Literal	Time is like an arrow.
Similar to	Time flies like an arrow.

- 光 represents day and 陰 represents night. Together, it means time in general.
- An arrow (矢)， like time, won't come back once unleashed.
- 如し *gotoshi* means "like" in a metaphoric sense; ～よう.

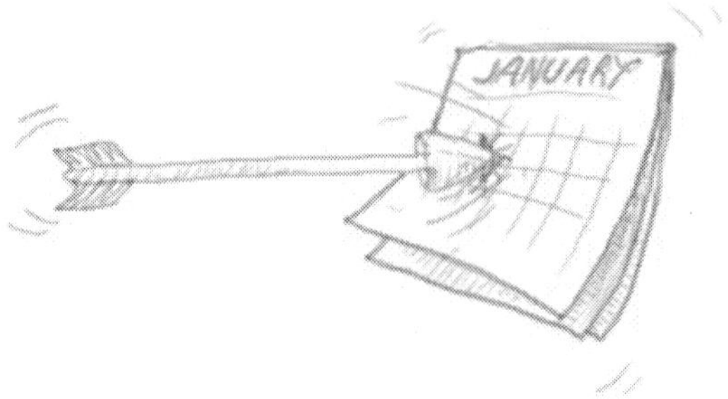

諺 光陰矢の如し

Time Flies Like an Arrow

ことし　おわ

もう今年も終わりか。

こういんや　ごと

光陰矢の如しだ。

mou kotoshi mo owari ka. kouin ya no gotoshi da.

This year is all but over. My, how time flies.

もう *mou*—already

今年 *kotoshi*—this year

も *mo*—also

終わりか *owari ka*—is over, huh? [the か emphasizes amazement of how fast the year had gone.]

諺 百聞は一見にしかず

Seeing is Believing

Japanese	ひゃくぶん　は　いっけんに　しかず *hyakubun wa ikken ni shikazu*
Literal	Hearing a hundred times is no match for seeing once.
Similar to	A picture is worth a thousand words; seeing is believing.

- 百聞 *hyakubun* listening a hundred times
- 一見 *ikken* a single look
- ～にしかず ~ *ni shikazu* no match for ~

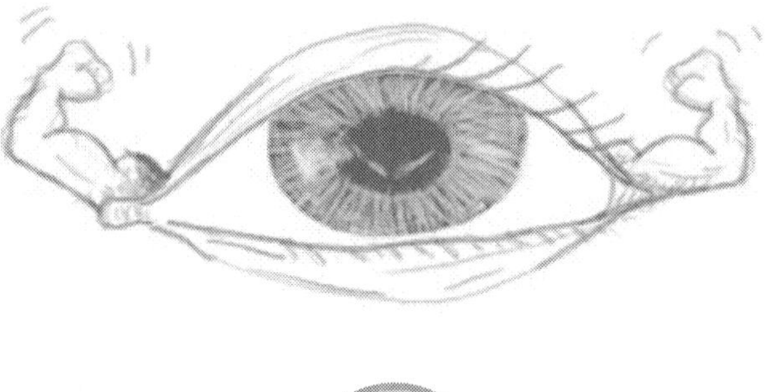

諺 百聞は一見にしかず

Seeing is Believing

いろいろ説明(せつめい)を聞(き)くよりも、実物(じつぶつ)をみよう。**百聞(ひゃくぶん)は一見(いっけん)にしかず**だ。

iroiro setsumei wo kiku yorimo, jitsubutsu wo miyou. hyakuben wa ikken ni shikazu da.

Instead of listening to countless explanations, let's see the real thing. Seeing is believing.

いろいろ *iroiro*—various

説明 *setsumei*—explanation

聞くよりも *kiku yorimo*—rather than listen...

実物 *jitsubutsu*—the real thing

みよう *miyou*—let's see...

諺 会うは別れの始め

The Best of Friends must Part

Japanese	あう　は　わかれ　の　はじめ *au wa wakare no hajime*
Literal	Meeting is the beginning of parting.
Similar to	The best of friends must part.

- 会う *au*—meeting
- 別れ *wakare*—parting
- ～の始め *no hajime*—the beginning of~

諺 会うは別れの始め

The Best of Friends must Part

空港(くうこう)で「**会(あ)うは別(わか)れの始(はじ)め**」と

いうことわざの意味(いみ)がわかった。

kuukou de "au wa wakare no hajime" to iu kotowaza no imi wakatta.

At the airport, I understood the old saying, "Meeting is the beginning of parting."

空港で *kuukou de*—at the airport
という *to iu*—such as; quotation marker
ことわざ *kotowaza*—proverb
意味 *imi*—meaning
わかった *wakatta*—understood

諺 頭隠して、尻隠さず

Hide Head, Leave Butt Exposed

Japanese	あたま　かくして、　しり　かくさず *atama kakushite, shiri kakusazu*
Literal	Hide head, don't hide butt
Similar to	Hiding your head in the sand (like an Ostrich)

- 隠して *kakushite*—hiding [The て form of 隠す *kakusu*—to hide; conceal]
- 隠さず *kakusazu*—not hide
- The ず is a negative ending.

諺 頭隠して、尻隠さず

Hide Head, Leave Butt Exposed

しんのすけは、かくれんぼをするとき、いつもおしりが見(み)えている。まさに、**頭隠(あたまかく)して尻隠(しりかく)さず**だ。

shinnosuke wa, kakurenbo wo suru toki, itsumo oshiri ga mieteiru. masa ni, atama kakushite shiri kakusazu da.

Shinnosuke when playing hide-and-go-seek, always (hides somewhere that) exposes his backend. Truly, this is hiding his head but not his butt.

しんのすけ *shinnosuke*—a boy's name
かくれんぼ *kakurenbo*—hide-and-go-seek (children's game)
するとき *suru toki*—when doing...
いつも *itsumo*—always
おしり *oshiri*—butt; backend
見えている *miete iru*—able to be seen
まさに *masa ni*—surely; certainly; truly

諺 自画自賛

Singing One's Own Praises

Japanese	じ が じ さん *ji ga ji san*
Literal	One's own picture; praising oneself
Similar to	Singing one's own Praises; tooting one's own Horn

- The 自 as you may guess adds the meaning of "oneself." You may know it from the common word 自分 *jibun* "oneself" and 自由 *jiyuu* "freedom."
- 画 *ga*—image; picture
- 賛 *san*—praise

諺 自画自賛

Singing One's Own Praises

じがじさん　き
自画自賛に聞こえるかもしれません

ほんとう　うた
が、ぼくは本当に歌がうまいよ。

jigajisan ni kikoeru kamoshiremasen ga, boku wa hontou ni uta ga umai yo.

It may sound like I'm bragging, but I'm really good at singing.

に聞こえる *ni kikoeru*—sounds like... [太くに見える *futoku ni mieru* - to look (appear) fat]
かもしれません *kamoshiremasen*—may; might; possibly
が *ga*—but
ぼく *boku*—I (usually used with males)
本当に *hontou ni*—really; truly (adv)
歌 *uta*—song [in this case singing in general]
うまい *umai*—good at; skillful; clever [can also be used with food or drink to mean "delicious"]

諺

右往左往

Running around like a chicken with its head cut off

Japanese	う おう さ おう *u ou sa ou*
Literal	Go right and left
Similar to	Running around like a chicken with its head cut off; go in all directions

- If you have trouble remembering right and left, just learn this and remember "right" goes first. Saying this fun phrase will help clear up the confusion. *u* (right) *ou sa* (left) *ou*
- 右折 *u setsu*—a right turn (often heard by car navigation systems)
- 左折 *sa setsu*—a left turn

諺 右往左往

Running around like a chicken with its head cut off

とつぜん　じしん　ひと
突然の地震で人々は
うおうさおう
右往左往した。

totsuzen no jishin de hitobito wa uousaou shita.

A sudden earthquake caused the people to go in all directions.

突然の *totsuzen no*—sudden; unexpected
地震 *jishin*—earthquake
人々 *hito bito*—people [The 々 shows repetition of the previous kanji: 人人; Note the sound change on the second "*hito*"]
した *shita*—Use する with 右往左往

諺 猿も木から落ちる

Even Monkeys fall from Trees

Japanese	さるも　き　から　おちる *saru mo ki kara ochiru*
Literal	Even monkeys fall from trees.
Similar to	Everyone makes mistakes.

- One of the most famous Japanese proverbs.
- 猿も *saru mo*—Even a Monkey
- 木から *ki kara*—from a tree
- 落ちる *ochiru*—to fall

諺 猿も木から落ちる

Even Monkeys fall from Trees

猿も木から落ちる(さる き お)というけど、あんなに賢(かしこ)い国語(こくご)の先生(せんせい)が、「一(いち)」という字(じ)を間違(まちが)えたなんて信(しん)じられない。

saru mo ki kara ochiru to iu kedo, anna ni kashikoi kokugo no sensei ga, ichi to iu ji wo machigaeta nante shijirarenai.

As they say, "Even monkeys fall from trees," but for such a brilliant Japanese teacher to mess up such a character is hard to believe.

という *to iu*— is like a quotation marker
けど *kedo*—but
あんなに *annani*—for such a
賢い *kashikoi*—wise; bright; clever
国語の先生 *kokugo no sensei*— teacher of Japanese
一 *ichi*—one; indisputably the easiest of all kanji
という *to iu*— is like a quotation marker
字 *ji*—character; here meaning Chinese characters
間違えた *machigaeta*—made a mistake
なんて *nante*—such as but with a negative emphasis
信じられない *shinjirarenai*—I can't believe it

諺 百年の恋も冷める

Even a Hundred Year Love can Turn Cold

Japanese	ひゃくねん　の　こい　も　さめる *hyakunen no koi mo sameru*
Literal	Even a hundred year old love can turn cold.
Similar to	Even a hundred year old love can turn cold.

- 百 *hyaku*—hundred
- 年 *nen*—year(s)
- の *no*—possessive marker
- 恋 *koi*—love
- も *mo*—also; even
- 冷める *sameru*—become cold

諺 百年の恋も冷める

Even a Hundred Year Love can Turn Cold

百年の恋も冷める瞬間。

ひゃくねん こい さ しゅんかん

hyaku nen no koi mo sameru shunkan.

The actual moment love grew cold...

瞬間 *shun kan*—moment lit. blink + space/time

諺 相手のない喧嘩はできぬ

It takes Two to Make a Quarrel

Japanese
あいてのない　けんか　は　できぬ
aite no nai kenka wa dekinu

Literal
You can't have a fight without the other person.

Similar to
It takes two to make a quarrel.

- 相手 *aite*—partner; someone else
- のない *no nai*—without; non-existent
- 喧嘩 *kenka*—quarrel; fight
- できぬ *dekinu*—can't [できない]

諺 相手のない喧嘩はできぬ

It takes Two to Make a Quarrel

あんたのせいじゃないか？

相手(あいて)のない喧嘩(けんか)はできぬ。

anta no sei janai ka? aite no nai kenka wa dekinu.

It isn't your fault? It takes two to tango.

あんた *anta*—you [a slightly rude shortened form of あなた *anata*]
～のせい ~ *no sei*—(your) fault [天気のせい *tenki no sei*—due to (the fault of) the weather]
じゃないか？ *janai ka*—it isn't (your fault)?!

諺 手を切る

To Wash one's Hands of a Matter

Japanese	てをきる *te wo kiru*
Literal	To cut a hand.
Similar to	To wash one's hands of a matter.

- This means to cut off all connections with something or someone.
- 手 *te*—hand
- を *wo*—(direct object marker)
- 切る *kiru*—to cut

諺 手を切る

To Wash one's Hands of a Matter

彼女(かのじょ)はあの男(おとこ)とは**手(て)を切(き)った。**

kanojo wa ano otoko to wa te wo kitta.

She cut off all relations with that guy.

彼女 *kanojo*—she ["he" is 彼 *kare*]
あの *ano*—that
男 *otoko*—man
と *to*—with (the man)
は *wa*—[topic marker]

諺 鉄は熱いうちに打て

Strike while the Iron is Hot

Japanese	てつ　は　あつい　うちに　うて *tetsu wa atsui uchi ni ute*
Literal	Strike while the iron is hot.
Similar to	Strike while the iron is hot.

- A rare case of a proverb literally meaning the same in Japanese and English.
- 鉄 *tetsu*—iron
- 熱い *atsui*—hot
- うちに *uchi ni*—while; during that time
- 打て *ute*—hit

諺 鉄は熱いうちに打て

Strike while the Iron is Hot

鉄(てつ)**は熱**(あつ)**いうちに打**(う)**て**！新入社員(しんにゅうしゃいん)にしっかり研修(けんしゅう)させよう。

tetsu wa atsui uchi ni ute! shinnyuu shain ni shikkari kenshuu saseyou.

Strike while the iron is hot! Let's get to the on-the-job training of the new employees.

新入 *shin nyuu*—newly arrived; newly joined
社員 *sha in*—company employee
しっかり *shikkari*—firmly; to (train) well
研修 *kenshuu*—training
させよう *saseyou*—to make someone do something

諺 一寸先は闇

No one Knows What the Future Holds

Japanese	いっすん　さき　は　やみ *issun saki wa yami*
Literal	One inch ahead is darkness.
Similar to	No one knows what the future holds.

- 一寸 *issun*—was a measurement approximately three centimeters in length. It can, as in this case, also mean "a little bit" of time as well as distance.
- 先 *saki*—ahead [Here, it refers to the future]
- 闇 *yami*—darkness; the dark [Like with English, this can also represent hopelessness and despair.]

諺 一寸先は闇
No one Knows What the Future Holds

かね
お金をしっかりためておこう。

いっすんさき　やみ
一寸先は闇だから。

okane wo shikkari tamete okou. issun saki wa yami dakara.

Let's save up our money. We don't know what the future holds.

お金 *okane*—money
しっかり *shikkari*—well; firmly
ためておこう *tamete okou*—let's save up
だから *dakara*—therefore; because of that

諺 時は金なり

Time is Money

Japanese	ときは　かね　なり *toki wa kane nari*
Literal	Time is money.
Similar to	Time is money.

- 時 *toki*—time; hour
- 金 *kane*—money; gold [In modern Japanese, 金 *kin* means "gold" and the honorific お *o* is added to mean money in general: お金 *okane*.]
- なり *nari*—an archaic ending meaning "to be."

諺 時は金なり

Time is Money

時(とき)は金(かね)なりだから、

しっかり勉強(べんきょう)して。

toki wa kane nari dakara, shikkari benkyou shite.

Time is money. Study hard.

しっかり *shikkari*—hard; do well
勉強 *benkyou*—study
して *shite*—do (study)

諺 うわさをすれば影

Speak of the Devil

Japanese	うわさ　を　すれば　かげ *uwasa wo sureba kage*
Literal	If you speak rumors, a shadow (will appear)
Similar to	Speak of the devil and he will appear.

- うわさ *uwasa*—gossip; rumor
- すれば *sureba*—if (you gossip)
- 影 *kage*—shadow (of the person spoken about)
- This is shortened from 噂をすれば影がさす *uwasa wo sureba kage ga sasu*—The first part is the same: "If you gossip..." but the 影がさす *kage ga sasu* means "to cast a shadow" or "to make an appearance."

諺 うわさをすれば影

Speak of the Devil

うわさをすれば影(かげ)。

あきこがきたわ。

uwasa wo sureba kage. akiko ga kita wa.

Speak of the devil. Here comes Akiko.

あきこ *akiko*—Akiko, a Japanese girl's name
きた *kita*—came [past tense of 来る *kuru*]
わ *wa*—a feminine sentence ender usually indicating emotion

諺 泣きっ面に蜂
Rub Salt in the Wound

Japanese	なきっつら　に　はち *nakittsura ni hachi*
Literal	To a crying face, a bee.
Similar to	Misfortunes seldom come alone.

- 泣く *naku*—to cry
- 面 *tsura*—face [other common readings are: おもて and めん]
- 泣きっ面 *nakittsura*—a crying face [Notice the small つ between the two compound words.]
- 蜂 *hachi*—bee

諺 泣きっ面に蜂

Rub Salt in the Wound

寝(ね)られない。起(お)きたら、レゴを踏(ふ)んだ。**泣(な)きっ面(つら)に蜂(はち)。**

nerarenai. okitara, rego wo funda. nakittsura ni hachi.

I couldn't sleep. Getting up, I stepped on a Lego. When it rains, it pours.

寝られない *nerarenai*—couldn't sleep [The 〜られない means **can't**]
起きたら *okitara*—upon getting up
レゴ *rego*—Lego piece [Any reader with children can sympathize.]
踏んだ *funda*—stepped on

諺	虎穴に入らずんば虎子を得ず Nothing Ventured, Nothing Gained

Japanese	こけつに　いらずんば　こじを えず *koketsu ni irazunba koshi wo ezu.*
Literal	If you don't enter the tiger's den, you won't get a baby tiger.
Similar to	Nothing ventured, nothing gained.

- If you don't take risks, you won't reap the rewards—in this case a baby tiger.
- 虎穴 *koketsu*—tiger's den; a dangerous place
- 入らずんば *irazunba*—if you don't go in
- 虎子 *koji* or *koshi*—a baby tiger
- 得ず *ezu*—won't aquire; won't get

諺 虎穴に入らずんば虎子を得ず

Nothing Ventured, Nothing Gained

じぎょう　はじ
事業を始めることはこわいけど、

こけつ　い　こじ　え
虎穴に入らずんば虎子を得ずだ。

jigyou wo hajimeru koto wa kowai kedo, koketsu ni irazunba koji wo ezu da.

Starting up a business is scary, but nothing ventured, nothing gained.

事業 *jigyou*—business
始めること *hajimeru koto*—the thing of beginning [the こと turns "to begin" into a noun phrase.]
こわい *kowai*—scary
けど *kedo*—but; however

諺 井の中の蛙大海を知らず

He that Stays in the Valley shall Never get Over the Hill.

Japanese	いのなかのかわずたいかいをしらず。 *i no naka no kawazu taikai wo shirazu.*
Literal	The frog in the well doesn't know the big ocean.
Similar to	He that stays in the valley shall never get over the hill.

- This is used for people who do not get out and live.
- 井 *i*—well
- 中 *naka*—inside [井の中 *i no naka*—in the well]
- 蛙 *kawazu*—frog [archaic pronunciation; frog today is かえる *kaeru*]
- 大海 *taikai*—the ocean; large sea
- 知らず *shirazu*—doesn't know

諺 井の中の蛙大海を知らず

He that Stays in the Valley shall Never get Over the Hill.

世間(せけん)知(し)らずにもほどがある。**井(い)の中(なか)の蛙(かわず)大海(たいかい)を知(し)らず**、ということかね。

seken shirazu ni mo hodo ga aru. i no naka no kawazu taikai wo shirazu, to iu koto ka ne.

I can’t believe you’re so clueless. You are like the frog in the well that knows nothing of the world.

世間 *seken*—world; society

知らず *shirazu*—ignorant of; doesn’t know

にもほどがある *ni mo hodo ga aru*—There’s a limit to... [This is an expression used to describe something indescribable, usually negatively. When you are shocked and have no words.]

ということ *to iu koto*—and that is that

かね *ka ne*—(question ender with the *ne* tag)

諺 好きこそものの上手なれ

What You Like to Do, You Will do Well

Japanese	すき　こそ　ものの　じょうず なれ *suki koso mono no jouzu nare*
Literal	Because you like something, you will become good at it.
Similar to	Who likes not his business, his business likes not him.

- This isn't quite "practice makes perfect" but you practice to perfection for a reason: you like the subject.
- 好き *suki*—to like
- こそ *koso*—for sure; for this reason
- もの *mono*—thing; matter; subject
- 上手 *jouzu*—good at
- なれ *nare*—to be [imperfect form of なり *nari* archaic for "to be."]

諺 好きこそものの上手なれ
What You Like to Do, You Will do Well

漢字(かんじ)が難(むずか)しい？漢字(かんじ)を趣味(しゅみ)として考(かんが)えたら。**好(す)きこそものの上手(じょうず)なれ。**

kanji ga muzukashii? kanji wo shumi toshite kangaetara. suki koso mono no jouzu nare.

Is kanji hard? Think of it as a hobby, because what you like to do, that you will do well.

漢字 *kanji*—kanji; Chinese characters in Japanese
難しい *muzukashii*—difficult; hard
趣味 *shumi*—hobby
として *toshite*—through; by
考えたら *kangaetara*—if you think

諺 蛙の子は蛙

The Apple Doesn't Fall Far from the Tree

Japanese かえる の こ は かえる
kaeru no ko wa kaeru

Literal The child of a frog is a frog.

Similar to Like hen, like chicken; the apple doesn't fall far from the tree

- 蛙 *kaeru*—frog [In some proverbs or old sayings the word for frog is かわず. This is an archaic form. Today, frog is always かえる. Basho's famous poem is 古池や蛙飛びこむ水の音 *furuike ya, kawazu tobikomu, mizu no oto*—an ancient pond, a frog jumps, the sound of water.]
- 蛙の子 *kaeru no ko*—baby frog [The word for tadpole is おたまじゃくし *otamajakushi*]

諺 蛙の子は蛙

The Apple Doesn't Fall Far from the Tree

父(ちち)のようにマークが犯罪者(はんざいしゃ)になった。**蛙(かえる)の子(こ)は蛙(かえる)。**

chichi no you ni ma-ku ga hanzaisha ni natta. kaeru no ko wa kaeru.

Just like his father, Mark has turned to crime. Like father, like son.

父 *chichi*—father
のように *no you ni*—just like; as
マーク *ma-ku*—Mark
犯罪者 *hanzaisha*—criminal
になった *ni natta*—became

諺 油断大敵

Idleness is the Devil's Workshop

Japanese	ゆ　だん　たい　てき *yu dan tai teki*
Literal	Negligence is a terrible enemy.
Similar to	Idleness is the devil's workshop; he that is too secure, isn't safe.

- 油断 *yudan*—negligence; unpreparedness [This is made up of 油 *abura*—oil and 断 *dan*—decision or judgment]
- 大敵 *taiteki*—a great enemy
- Adding 大 (*dai* or *tai*) before many nouns make it bigger:
  大反対 *dai hantai*—strong opposition
  大成功 *dai seikou*—a great success
  大失敗 *dai shippai*—a terrible failure

諺 油断大敵

Idleness is the Devil's Workshop

ゆだんたいてき
油断大敵だよ。

しょうり
まだ勝利してない。

yudantaiteki da yo. mada shouri shitenai.

Don't be overconfident. We haven't won yet.

よ *yo*—sentence ender for emphasis
まだ *mada*—yet
勝利 *shouri*—victory
してない *shitenai*—haven't

諺 足が出る

Run over Budget

Japanese	あし　が　でる *ashi ga deru*
Literal	Foot is sticking out.
Similar to	To not cover expenses.

- 足 *ashi*—leg; foot
- 出る *deru*—to extend; to come forth
- Other 足 idioms include:
  足が棒になる *ashi ga bou ni naru*—to walk so much your leg turns into a stick.
  足を引っ張る *ashi wo hipparu*—literally “to pull someone’s legs” but doesn’t mean what that means in English. 足を引っ張る means to slow someone down—to be a drag on someone.

諺 足が出る

Run over Budget

今月(こんげつ)も**足(あし)が出(で)た**。お金(かね)に気(き)を付(つ)けて。

kongetsu mo ashi ga deta. okane ni ki wo tsukete.

We ran over budget again this month. Be careful with the money.

今月 *kongetsu*—this month [今年 *kotoshi*—this year (notice, it is not "*kontoshi*"); 今回 *konkai*—this time; 今週 *konshuu*—this week]
も *mo*—also
お金 *okane*—money
気を付けて *ki wo tsukete*—be careful

諺 笑う門には福来たる

Fortune will Come to the Home of Those who Smile.

Japanese	わらう かど には ふく きたる *warau kado niwa fuku kitaru*
Literal	Good fortune comes to the home of those smile.
Similar to	Fortune comes in by a merry gate.

- 笑う *warau*—to laugh; to smile
- 門 *kado*—gate; entrance to a home
- には *ni wa*—に *ni*, the particle showing the direction of the action (to the laughing house) + は *wa*, the topic particle.
- 福 *fuku*—good fortune
- 来たる *kitaru*—to come; to arrive

諺 笑う門には福来たる

Fortune will Come to the Home of Those who Smile.

わる　　　　　　　　わら
悪いことがあっても、笑って。

わら　かど　　　ふく き
笑う門には福来たるだから。

warui koto ga attemo, waratte. warau kado niwa fuku kitaru dakara.

Even when bad things happen, laugh. As they say, fortune will come to the home of those who smile.

悪いこと *warui koto*—a bad thing
[悪い *warui*—bad + こと *koto*—thing]
あっても *attemo*—even if occurs
笑って *waratte*—(you) laugh; smile
だから *dakara*—therefore

諺 知らぬが仏

Ignorance is Bliss

Japanese	しらぬ が ほとけ *shiranu ga hotoke*
Literal	Ignorance is Buddha.
Similar to	Ignorance is bliss.

- This proverb means if you knew some particular information, you might get upset or worry. Not knowing, you can remain peaceful and calm.
- 知らぬ *shiranu*—don't know
- 仏 *hotoke*—Buddha
  [This is also the character for France: 仏 *futsu*]

諺 知らぬが仏

Ignorance is Bliss

お父(とう)さんはかなり大(おお)きい借金(しゃっきん)が

あるらしいけど、娘(むすめ)は

知(し)らないんだ。**知(し)らぬが仏(ほとけ)**。

otousan wa kanari ookii shakkin ga aru rashii kedo, musume wa shiranain da. shiranu ga hotoke.

Sounds like her father has quite a lot of debt, but the daughter doesn't know about it. Knowledge is bliss.

お父さん *otousan*—father
かなり *kanari*—fairly; considerably
大きい *ookii*—big; large
謝金 *shakin*—debt
らしい *rashii*—sounds like; it seems
けど *kedo*—but; however
娘 *musume*—daughter

諺 安物買いの銭失い

You Get What you Pay For

Japanese	やすもの　がい　の　ぜに　うしない *yasumono gai no zeni ushinai*
Literal	Buying cheap things is a waste of money.
Similar to	You get what you pay for.

- 安物 *yasumono*—something cheap
- 買い *gai*—purchase; something bought
- 銭 *zeni*—a hundredth of a yen
- 失い *ushinai*—to lose
- 銭失い *zeni ushinai*—a waste of money

諺 安物買いの銭失い

You Get What you Pay For

これはたったの五十円(ごじゅうえん)だったけど、もう壊(こわ)れた。**安物(やすもの)買(が)いの銭(ぜに)失(うしな)い。**

kore wa tatta no gojuuen datta kedo, mou kowareta. yasumono gai no zeni ushinai.

This was only fifty yen and is already broken. You get what you pay for.

これは *kore wa*—as for this
たったの *tatta no*—just; only
五十円 *gojuu en*—fifty yen
だった *datta*—was
けど *kedo*—but; however
もう *mou*—already
壊れた *kowareta*—broken

諺 論より証拠

The Proof is in the Pudding

Japanese	ろん　より　しょうこ *ron yori shouko*
Literal	Evidence is better than debate.
Similar to	The proof of the pudding is in the eating.

- This is one of the sayings found in the 江戸いろはかるた *edo iroha karuta* card game.
- 論 *ron*—argument; discussion
- より *yori*—instead of this
- 証拠 *shouko*—evidence

諺 論より証拠
The Proof is in the Pudding

きょう
今日のテストをみせて。

ろん　しょうこ
論より証拠。

kyou no tesuto wo misete. ron yori shouko.

(Mother speaking) Show me today's test. The proof is in the pudding.

If your son or daughter tries to assure you they aced their test, this example sentence may come in handy.

今日の *kyou no*—today's [The の makes the possessive.]

テスト *tesuto*—test

みせて *misete*—show me [みる *miru*—to see; みせて *misete*—show me]

諺 情けは人の為ならず

Compassion is not for Other People's Benefit

Japanese	なさけ は ひと の ため ならず *nasake wa hito no tame narazu*
Literal	Compassion isn't only for the benefit of others.
Similar to	One good turn deserves another; a kindness is never lost.

- The good you do for others is the good you do for yourself.
- 情け *nasake*—compassion; sympathy
- 人 *hito*—(other) person
- 為 *tame*—benefit; welfare; sake
- ならず *narazu*—won't be; should not be

諺 情けは人の為ならず

Compassion is not for other people's benefit

彼(かれ)は知(し)らない人(ひと)にお金(かね)を貸(か)して
あげたら、お給料(きゅうりょう)が上(あ)がった
わ。**情(なさ)けは人(ひと)の為(ため)ならず**ね。

kare wa shiranai hito ni okane wo kashite agetara, okyuuryou ga agatta wa. nasake wa hito no tame narazu ne.

He gave some money to a stranger and now he got a raise. One good turn deserves another.

彼 *kare*—he
知らない人 *shiranai hito*—a stranger
お金 *okane*—money
貸してあげたら *kashite agetara*—gave; loaned
お給料 *okyuuryou*—salary
上がったわ *agatta wa*—raised + feminine sentence ender *wa.*

諺 嘘から出た実

Many a True Word is Spoken in Jest

Japanese	うそ　から　でた　まこと *uso kara deta makoto*
Literal	From a lie appeared the truth.
Similar to	Many a true word is spoken in jest.

- This is also sometimes said as 嘘より出たまこと *uso yori deta makoto.*
- 嘘 *uso*—a lie
- から *kara*—from (a lie)
- でた *deta*—came out; appeared
- 実 *makoto*—truth [This kanji, meaning "truth," often has the pronunciation of じつ and can also mean "fruit" as in the fruit of a tree.]

諺 嘘から出た実

Many a True Word is Spoken in Jest

うそ で まこと かのじょ ほんとう

嘘から出た実で、彼女は本当に

かね も

お金持ちになった。

uso kara deta makoto de, kanojo wa hontou ni okane mochi ni natta.

After joking about being rich, she really did become wealthy.

で *de*—by; with; by means of
彼女 *kanojo*—she
本当に *hontou ni*—really; truly
お金持ち *okanemochi*—wealthy
になった *ni natta*—became

FREE EXTRA RESOURCES

To get a download that includes recordings of all the proverbs and their examples sentences—both slow and normal speeds—and a PDF for printing the book, please type the following URL in the browser on your computer:

http://TheJapanesePage.com/downloads/kotowaza.zip

Please do not share this link, but we would love it if the download will help you with your learning. We've put in a lot of effort to make this product. If you have any problems with the download or have any other questions, please email us at **help@thejapanshop.com.**

We'd love to hear from you!

どうもありがとうございました！